FITTING TACK

by

Jane Holderness-Roddam

Illustrations by

Carole Vincer

KENILWORTH PRESS

First published in Great Britain by
The Kenilworth Press Limited,
Addington, Buckingham, MK18 2JR

© The Kenilworth Press Limited 1987

Reprinted 1987, 1988, 1990, 1991, 1992, 1993

British Library Cataloguing in Publication Data
A catalogue record for this book is available from the British Library.

ISBN 0-901366-43-9

Typeset by Falcon Graphic Art Ltd

Printed in Great Britain by Westway Offset

CONTENTS

Introduction

Over the centuries a vast collection of tack has been evolved and refined for horses and ponies. This book sets out to explain the basics of correct and comfortable tack fitting whilst pointing out the most common faults and showing how to avoid them. Beginning with the halter and headcollar for leading, it goes on to cover snaffle and double bridles, nosebands, the most commonly used bits and martingales, the saddle and its attachments and more specialist equipment such as breastplates, weight cloths, cruppers and lungeing tackle.

Since good quality tack is a sound investment that should last a lifetime, it makes sense to look after it. The maintenance and care of tack is therefore also included here, along with safety tips where appropriate.

The type and conformation of your horse, the way in which he moves and the kind of work you wish to do all have a bearing on the most suitable type of tack. While a neat and elegant bridle will be required for showing, a broader stronger one will be best for jumping, cross-country and all-purpose uses. It is worthwhile spending some time when choosing your tack to make sure that you find the best type for you and your horse.

There are bridles, saddles and gadgets for every type of horse, but simplicity should always be the aim. Whether you are a novice or more experienced rider, stick to the equipment that is essential, making sure that it is well cared for and correctly fitted.

Halters and headcollars

A **halter**, usually made of rope or rope and webbing, acts as a combination of headcollar and lead rope to lead or tie up a horse. To fit, put the rope round the horse's neck, loosen the noseband and pass it over the muzzle, then take the headpiece over the ears. Adjust the halter to the right size at either side of the nose and tie a knot, as shown, to secure it.

Headcollars are normally made of leather or nylon and are available in several sizes. They fasten at the headpiece, though some may also be adjusted at the noseband. Some headcollars have a browband which must be straightened around the ears and under the forelock.

For leading or tying up, a clip rope is attached to the ring at the back of the noseband.

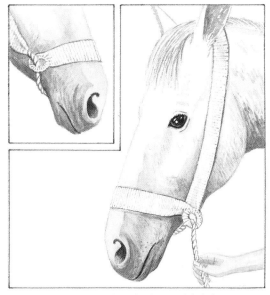

A rope and webbing **halter** which has been loosened and put on over the nose and the head. It can be adjusted for size on the offside.

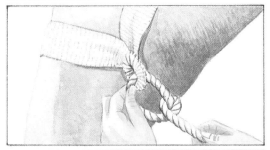

A knot must always be tied, as shown, to prevent injury to the jaw should the horse get caught up or pull back.

The **headcollar** in place. Take care not to flick the headpiece in the horse's eye as it passes over the poll. The spring clip on the rope should face backwards.

Putting on a snaffle bridle

The **snaffle** is the simplest and most common bridle. It consists of a headpiece and throatlash, browband, cheekpieces attached to the headpiece and bit, reins and a noseband.

Make sure that it is adjusted to the correct size and that the noseband and throatlash are undone before you put it on. Once in place, do up the buckles, starting from the top and working down: throatlash then noseband.

Check all the straps are through their keepers and runners. To remove: undo noseband then throatlash.

Place the reins over the head and draw the bridle up as shown. Guide the bit with the left hand and open the mouth by feeling into the corners with the fingers.

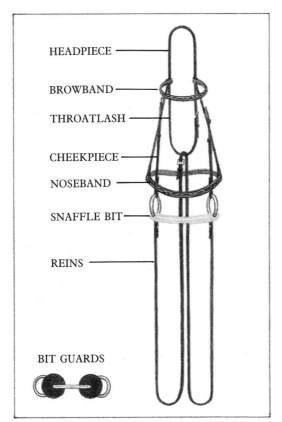

HEADPIECE

BROWBAND

THROATLASH

CHEEKPIECE

NOSEBAND

SNAFFLE BIT

REINS

BIT GUARDS

Snaffle bridle with decorative stitching and rubber straight-bar bit. Inset: bit with rubber bit guards to prevent soreness at the corners of the mouth.

Alternative method: hold the bridle in the right hand, crooked under the jaw and over the nose. Ease the mouth open as before.

Take the bridle over the head, easing the ears through one at a time. Check that the bridle fits, and adjust the cheekpieces if necessary.

Straighten the bridle, check that everything is in position, pull the forelock over the browband, and adjust the mane under the headpiece.

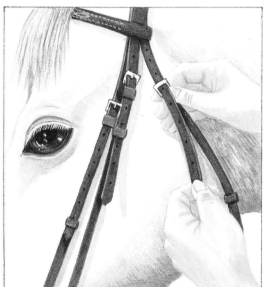

The throatlash must not restrict breathing, so when fastening it remember that some horses become very thick through the jaw in collected paces.

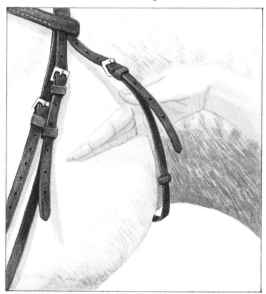

The flat of your hand should fit between the jaw and throatlash when it is roughly the correct length. Push the keepers home.

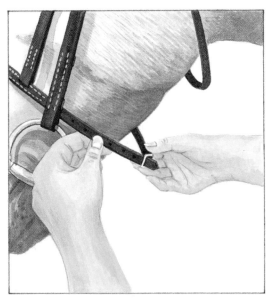

A cavesson noseband like this is fastened on the inside of the cheekpieces. Check that both sides are level and allow two fingers' freedom on the nose.

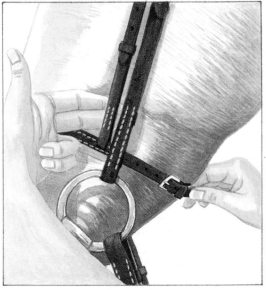

The cavesson should lie about two fingers' breadth below the prominent cheekbones to avoid chafing. If it is too low it will pinch against the bit.

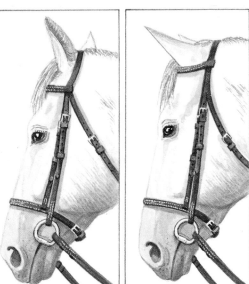

Browbands must not be so tight that they pinch the back of the ears, or so high that they rub around the base of them. Discomfort can cause head shaking.

If the horse is to be left tacked up or lunged, the reins can be crossed and looped over the head. A headcollar or lunge cavesson can be fitted on top.

Bits

The choice of bit is vital to the way the horse responds and behaves with the rider. The mildest are the thick **loose ringed** or **eggbutt** (fixed ring) **snaffles**. As the horse's mouth is extremely sensitive, some are more comfortable in a **rubber** or **vulcanite** bit or a **half-moon** or **straight bar** without the 'nutcracker' action of a joint. Others may go better in a **double jointed** bit which is straight in the middle. If a horse does not turn easily, a **cheek snaffle** will help by accentuating the pressure on the cheeks and preventing the bit from being pulled through the mouth.

Rubber and copper bits, although softer, will deteriorate in time, and must be checked regularly. A stainless steel (not nickel) bit should last a lifetime.

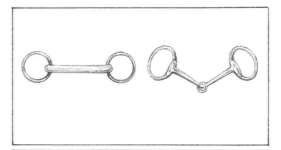

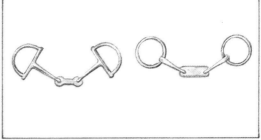

Four different types of snaffle. *Top left*: **straight bar** with loose rings, *right*: plain **jointed eggbutt**; *below left*: **double-jointed D-ring**; *right*: **Dr Bristol**.

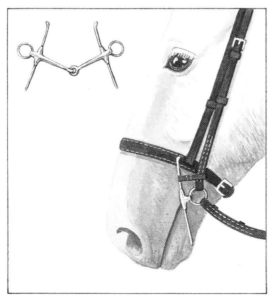

Cheek snaffle showing leather keepers to hold it upright. The cheeks are a steering aid and stop the bit rings being pulled through the mouth.

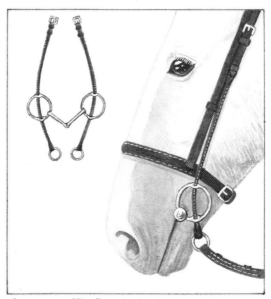

A **gag snaffle** fitted with its own cheek pieces. This severe snaffle acts on the poll and the mouth and requires sympathetic handling.

Fitting a snaffle bit

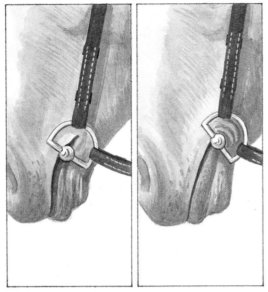

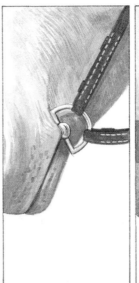

If fitted too low (*left*) the bit may knock against the teeth and encourage the horse to put his tongue over it. Too high (*right*) will be uncomfortable.

Too narrow a bit (*left*) will press into the cheeks, causing bruising and soreness. Too wide (*right*) and it will be unable to act correctly.

Pelham

The **pelham** is a combination of snaffle and curb, with a single mouthpiece, It is useful for horses who are too strong in a snaffle but find the two bits of a double uncomfortable. The mouthpiece may be half moon, straight or jointed; metal, rubber or vulcanite.

Two methods of using a pelham. *Left*, with two reins, *right*, with roundings and a single rein, which makes it easy to use but rather defeats the action of the bit.

Kimblewick

The **Kimblewick** is a variation of the pelham. The square eye which attaches it to the cheekpieces has a downward action on the poll to help lower the head. If the rein can be set low on the bit 'D' a greater leverage is exerted. Only use it with a cavesson noseband.

Two types of Kimblewick. The slotted bit rings, *left*, allow different degrees of control. The curved mouthpiece gives extra room for the tongue.

Nosebands

Several nosebands are available which have been designed to accentuate the action of the bit in various ways. The mildest and most common is the **cavesson**. This is the only noseband used with a double bridle or a standing martingale.

The **drop** noseband, designed to prevent the horse from opening its mouth to evade or resist the aids, helps with control. It is positioned slightly lower on the nose than the cavesson but must not restrict the breathing in any way. The strap is fastened below the bit, resting in the chin groove, and should be tight enough to stop the horse opening his mouth without being uncomfortable. Never attach a standing martingale to a drop.

When buying a drop noseband choose a broad nosepiece for comfort, and check that the rings at either side of the nose have metal spikes set into the cheekpieces. These prevent the noseband from drooping downwards and hampering the horse's breathing.

The **flash** and **grakle** are a combination of cavesson and drop nosebands, though they have slightly different actions. A standing martingale can be used with the cavesson part of the flash but not with a grakle. The latter is particularly useful for a horse who crosses his jaw.

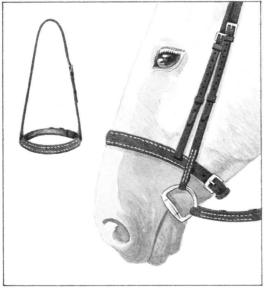

The **cavesson** is the traditional style of noseband. It may be used with any kind of bit or a standing martingale. The nosepiece can vary considerably in width.

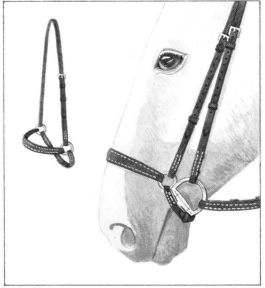

A **drop** noseband is used for horses who open or cross their jaws. The back strap goes under the bit. The front should not press on the nostrils. Use only with a snaffle.

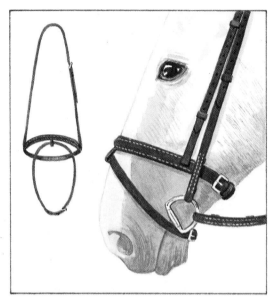

A **flash** noseband combines a cavesson and a drop. A standing martingale can be attached to the cavesson. Keep the buckle at the back, to prevent rubbing.

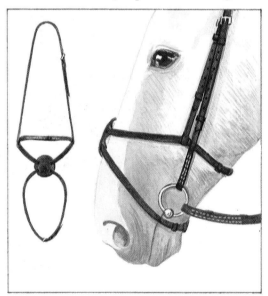

The **grakle** is useful for preventing the horse crossing his jaw. It should be comfortably tight with the cross central and the straps not tight on the cheeks.

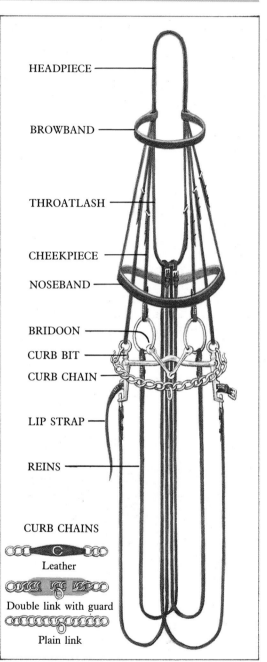

HEADPIECE

BROWBAND

THROATLASH

CHEEKPIECE

NOSEBAND

BRIDOON

CURB BIT

CURB CHAIN

LIP STRAP

REINS

CURB CHAINS

Leather

Double link with guard

Plain link

Double bridle with reins attached both to bridoon and curb bits. A variety of curb chains can be used. The choice will depend on the horse and his way of going.

Double bridle

As its name implies, the **double bridle** has two bits. The snaffle or bridoon raises the head. The curb with a curb chain determines the degree of control and has a lowering effect. This is a sophisticated bridle which requires considerable skill on the part of the rider.

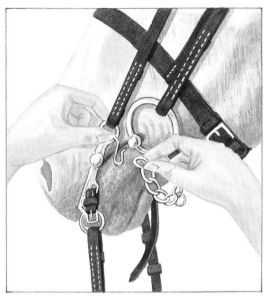

Take the chain from under the bridoon on the off side and, keeping it flat, place it over the hook beneath the bit ring on the near side.

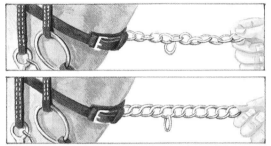

The curb chain must be turned until it lies flat against the chin, with the loose link hanging underneath.

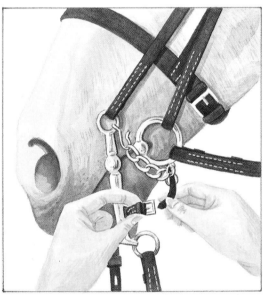

Thread the lip strap through the central link and fasten it through the keeper. Its function is to hold the chain in place.

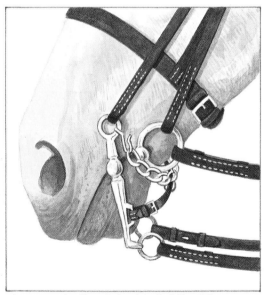

A correctly fitted double bridle. There should be a 45° angle on the curb cheek when the chain is fastened and there is contact on the rein.

Saddles

The saddle is the most expensive item of tack, and it must fit correctly and comfortably. A good saddle, properly cared for, will last a lifetime so it is well worth getting an expert's opinion to help you choose the right one.

Saddles are made up round a frame known as the 'tree'. They generally come in three widths – narrow, medium and broad – and different lengths to suit the horse's back.

There are three principal designs of saddle: dressage, jumping and general purpose riding. The **dressage saddle** is very straight-cut, with the stirrup bar positioned well back to allow for the long leg position. The **jumping saddle** with a forward-cut flap and corresponding stirrup bar allows for the shorter stirrups used for jumping. The **general purpose saddle** is a combination of the two, and is eminently suitable for all types of riding, including cross-country.

The parts of the saddle are: pommel, waist, seat, cantle, flaps, sometimes sweat flaps, panels, girth straps to which the girths are attached, girth buckle guards to protect the flaps getting worn by the girth buckles, and stirrup bars to which the leathers and stirrup irons are fixed. The gullet is the channel between the two panels, which must be wide enough for the horse's spine.

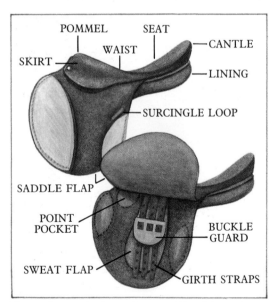

Two views of a **jumping saddle**. Note the forward-cut design and padded knee-rolls to accommodate the short, jumping length stirrups.

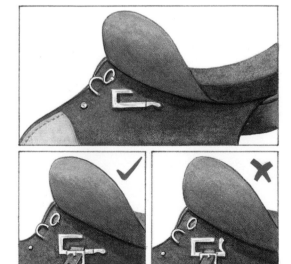

The **stirrup bar** in the open position. It should never be closed with a rider in the saddle, as a fixed stirrup leather could trap him in a fall.

Girths, stirrup irons and leathers

There are three main types of **girth**. **Webbing** is always used in pairs, as a single girth could break. **String** or **nylon** are strong and help to prevent galling. **Leather**, although it is the most expensive, lasts a long time if cared for properly. When buying, consider quality of material, stitching and strength. Wider girths are more comfortable than narrow ones. Elasticated inserts give greater flexibility but must be of double strength, as single ones are not strong enough.

Stirrup irons should be big enough to hold the width of the foot with ½" on either side. Too large and the whole foot could slip through. Too small and the foot could be trapped. Rubbers inserted into the base of the iron will give extra grip. Leathers must fit the iron and be the right length for the rider.

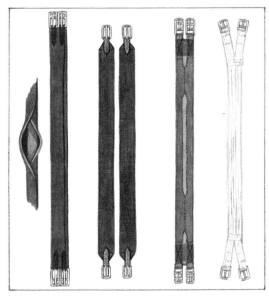

Some of the most common **girths**. *Left to right*: **leather threefold** with oiled strip inside to keep it supple. **Webbing** used as a pair. Foam filled **nylon** and **string**.

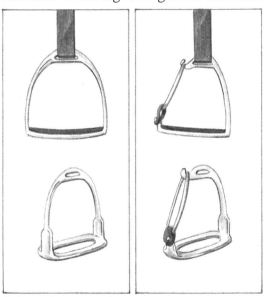

Stirrup irons. *Left*, an ordinary stirrup with and without a rubber. *Right*, a **safety iron** with rubber ring on the outside which will slip off if the rider falls.

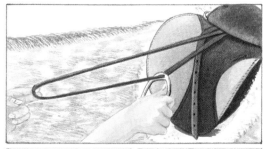

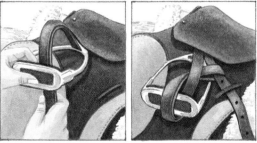

Stirrup irons should never be left dangling, in case they frighten the horse or get caught. Run them up to secure, folding the leather through for extra security.

Putting on a saddle

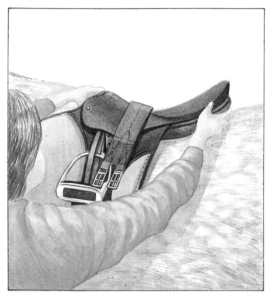

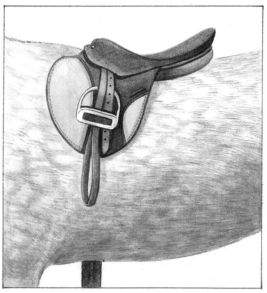

Girths are attached on the offside and folded over the saddle with stirrups run up. The saddle is placed on the withers and slipped back so that the hair is flat underneath.

With the saddle in position, the girths are dropped gently over. If the horse is young or nervous, the girths should be lifted down from the offside.

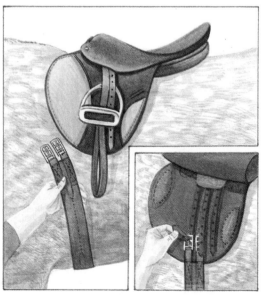

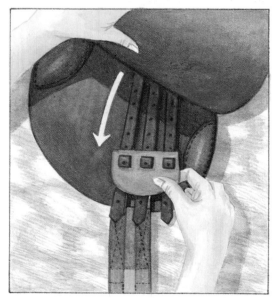

Girths are fastened on the first two, or first and third, girth straps. With two girths, the inside one goes on the front strap, the outside on the second.

Check that the buckles are level. Pull the buckle guard down to protect the flap. Always check girths before and after mounting as they may need adjusting.

Fitting a saddle

It is important for a saddle to fit correctly, otherwise it will cause discomfort and eventual injury to the horse's back. The main points to check with a rider in position are:

1 The saddle must be the right size for horse and rider.

2 There must be (a) no pressure on the horse's spine and (b) a clear channel through the gullet.

3 The tree must not press on or pinch the withers.

4 The saddle must rest level and distribute the rider's weight evenly without cramping the shoulder movement or resting too far back on the loins.

A saddle can be re-stuffed periodically to improve the panels, but a different saddle is the only real solution if the tree does not fit a particular horse.

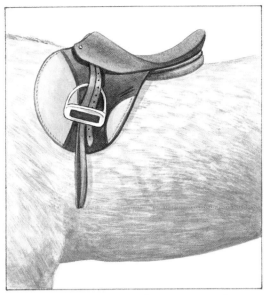

A saddle which is out of balance, resting too high on the horse and pushing the rider's weight back into a concentrated area.

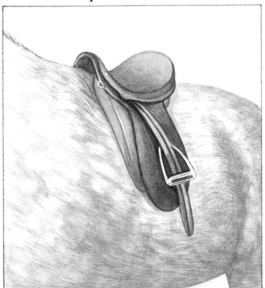

Here the tree is too narrow and is pinching the withers. This will cause pressure and will restrict the free movement of the shoulders.

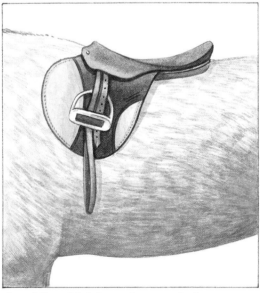

A saddle which is too low on the horse. This could be remedied by re-stuffing, but the tree may still be too wide for the horse's back.

Martingales

Martingales are used to prevent the horse from raising his head too high and out of the angle of control. The **standing martingale** consists of a strap running from the noseband through a neckstrap and down between the front legs to the girth. It should act when the head is too high. Standing martingales must only be used with a cavesson noseband to avoid restricting the breathing or damaging the nose.

The **running martingale** divides into two branches at the neckstrap. These end in rings through which the reins pass, helping to stop the horse from raising his head too high or throwing it from side to side, and also improving steerage. **Stops** must be fitted to the reins to prevent the rings from catching on the buckles or billets near the bit.

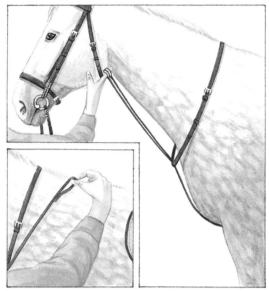

The neckstrap is placed over the head and the lower end is secured to the girth. Check the correct length by taking the top end up to the gullet or withers.

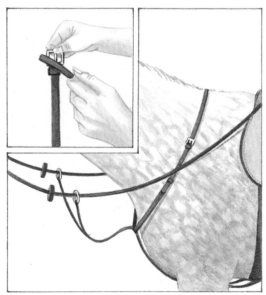

Rubber stops should be placed on both reins between the bit and the rings of a **running martingale**, to prevent them catching on the rein buckles.

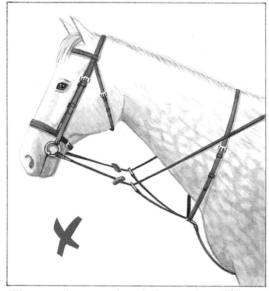

The running martingale is too short if it pulls the reins downwards out of their natural line when the horse's head is in the normal position.

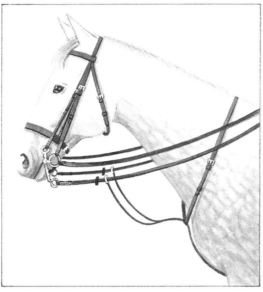

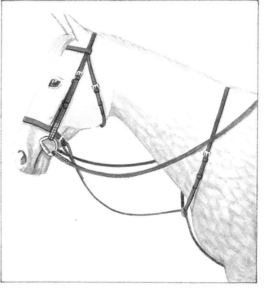

If a running martingale is used with a double bridle it is placed on the curb reins to accentuate their lowering action. Stops must always be used.

A **standing martingale** fitted correctly with a cavesson noseband. A rubber stop secures the neckstrap and prevents it slipping forward.

Numnahs

A **numnah** is a shaped pad usually made of sheepskin, synthetic fleece, felt, cotton or nylon. It helps relieve pressure on the horse's back but should only be used as an emergency measure if the saddle does not fit correctly. It must be 1″ larger than the saddle all round.

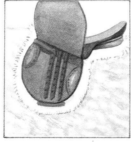

A numnah in position. The strap is fitted over one of the girth straps to hold it in place. The girth may fasten through the lower loop for greater security.

The numnah must be pulled well up into the front arch of the saddle to avoid pressure on the withers. It may be attached to the saddle before tacking up.

Breastplates and breast girths

Breastplates and breast girths are designed to prevent the saddle from slipping back, especially on a fit, lean horse. The **hunting breastplate** consists of a neckstrap attached to the saddle 'D's' on either side of the withers and to the girth between the forelegs.

A standing or running martingale attachment can be added to the front breast ring if required.

The racing-type **breast girth** is a strap made from webbing, leather or elastic, which fits across the chest and attaches to the girth straps on either side. It must not be so high that it hinders neck movement nor so low that it restricts the shoulders.

A **surcingle** will hold the breast girth in place on the saddle.

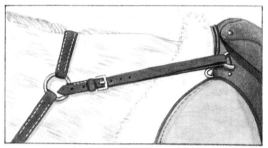

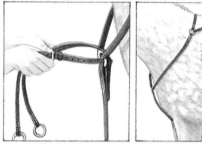

A **breastplate** in position. It should be comfortable but tight enough to prevent the saddle slipping. *Left*: breastplate with martingale attachment.

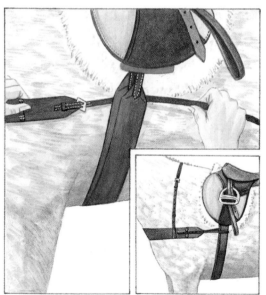

The **breast girth** is attached to the girth on either side of the neck. It should not be tight or low around the shoulders or high enough to press into the neck.

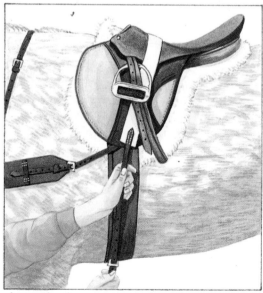

A **surcingle** or **over-girth** will stop the saddle flaps wrinkling or the breast girth straps moving. It should buckle under the belly centrally, avoiding the elbows.

Weight cloth

A **weight cloth** is required for advanced eventing, jumping or racing. There are several different styles, but all should distribute the lead evenly on either side of the horse's spine, with rather more to the front near the centre of balance but not pressing on the withers.

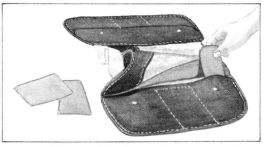

This weight cloth is shaped to the horse's back and has no securing straps. The weights are placed evenly in the pockets and kept forward as much as possible.

The weight cloth is best placed over a numnah, unless it is already padded. Both should be pulled well into the front arch before tightening the girths.

Crupper

A **crupper** is fastened under the tail and used to stop the saddle from sliding forward. It is particularly useful for fat ponies without much wither. As cruppers are not as common as they used to be you may have to ask a saddler to fit a 'D' on the back of the saddle.

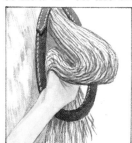

This crupper has no buckles, so the tail is pulled through gently. When using a crupper for the first time, have a helper to hold the pony.

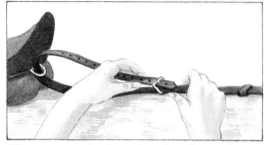

The crupper (*top*) can be placed round the tail and fastened in place. Fasten the other end to the 'D' on the saddle, just tight enough not to pull the tail up.

Lungeing equipment

Lungeing consists of circling a horse round the handler on a long rein attached to a headpiece. Its function is to exercise or train the horse. Equipment for lungeing includes: a **lungeing cavesson**, which is a headpiece with three rings on the noseband; **lunge rein**, about seven metres long; **side reins**, attached from the saddle or roller to the cavesson or bridle; and a **lunge whip**. The horse should always be protected with boots or bandages, and the handler should wear gloves and a hard hat.

For exercising purposes, a cavesson, lunge rein and whip are all that is needed. Side reins give greater control and encourage the horse to go forward into an even contact with a natural head carriage. A knowledgeable handler may also use them with a bridle.

If a saddle is used, the stirrups should be removed or fastened up. A surcingle will secure the flaps if the horse is nervous.

When a bridle is used, the noseband should be removed to allow room for the cavesson which fits inside the cheekpieces. The reins can be twisted together and threaded through the throatlash or crossed and looped over the neck to secure them.

Side reins should be clipped together and attached to the 'D' rings on the saddle when leading the horse to the lungeing area.

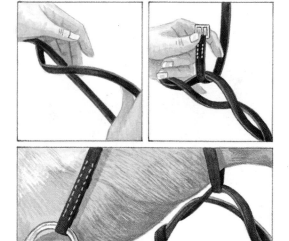

If lungeing with a bridle, the reins can be removed altogether or secured out of the way by twisting and fastening with the throatlash.

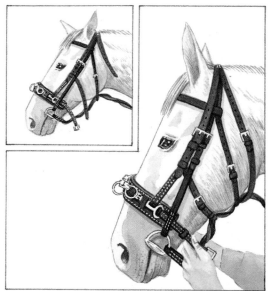

The cavesson is placed over the bridle and fastened under the cheekpieces. It is usually best to remove the noseband from the bridle.

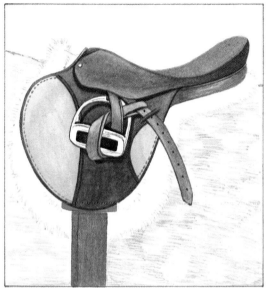

When lungeing with a saddle, it is important to secure the irons so that they will not flap around. If they look like working loose they should be removed.

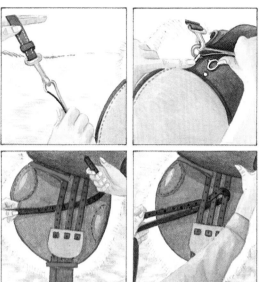

Side reins are usually threaded through the girth straps above the buckles to keep them in place. When not in use, they should be attached to the saddle 'Ds'.

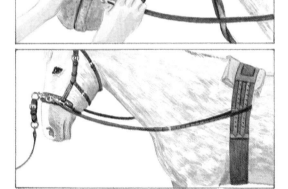

The lunge rein is fixed to the middle ring on the cavesson and the side reins to the rings on either side. Here, a roller is being used instead of a saddle.

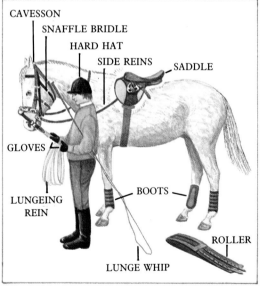

CAVESSON
SNAFFLE BRIDLE
HARD HAT
SIDE REINS
SADDLE
GLOVES
LUNGEING REIN
BOOTS
ROLLER
LUNGE WHIP

A horse ready for lungeing, showing all the necessary equipment.

Care of tack

Correct care of tack undoubtedly prolongs its life. Regular checks on all stitching and the condition of the leather is also essential for safety. All tack should be sponged off and wiped over every time it is used, then dismantled once a week and cleaned thoroughly to keep it in good order.

Begin by rubbing over the leather with a damp towelling cloth or sponge, then work saddle soap into both sides of the leather, paying special attention to folds and bends. If the leather feels hard, apply neatsfoot oil or a similar leather preservative with a small brush or sponge. Once it has been absorbed, rub in saddle soap liberally. Pay particular attention to the condition of the leather on the reins, which may become worn and thin round the bit, and also girth straps and stirrup leathers. Check the stitching on the saddle and attend to any signs of wear immediately before the tack becomes unsafe.

Metal work should be washed in warm water and dried carefully. Metal polish can be applied to give it a shine, but avoid using it on mouthpieces, as it has an unpleasant taste. Be careful, too, that you do not transfer the polish to the leather work, as it will leave a white mark. If rubbers are used in the stirrup irons, remove them and wash and dry them before replacing.

Girths made of webbing, string or nylon should be brushed off after use and given a chance to dry and air. Wash them if necessary, but not in strong soap powders or detergents, which might cause a skin reaction in the horse. Leather girths should be kept soft and pliable. The threefold variety will contain a strip of oiled blanket for this purpose.

Numnahs should be clean, dry and soft. Once they become rough they can cause a sore back and defeat their purpose. Regular brushing with a stiff brush, or combing with a plastic curry comb if they are the sheepskin variety, will keep them soft. Many can be washed in a machine, but sheepskin is best washed by hand, allowed to dry naturally, and then oiled if necessary.

When storing tack, avoid a hot atmosphere as this will dry out the leather, or damp conditions which will quickly result in a growth of mildew.